READABLE
Poetry and Prose

DMTAKESHI

© 2024 Readable / Unreadable; A Poetry Collection
Author: DM Takeshi
Editor: Brandy Lane
Cover design: Brandy Lane
Foreword: Sara J and Billie J

All rights reserved.
Printed in the United States of America.

No part of this book may be used, stored in a system retrieval system, or transmitted, in any form or any means—by electronic, mechanical, photocopying, recording, or reproduced in any manner whatsoever—without written permission from the author, except in the case of brief quotations embodied in critical articles and reviews.

ISBN: 978-1-7363268-9-3
Library of Congress Control Number: 2024917941

Published in the United States of America by:
Where Beautiful Inks LLC
Fort Wayne, Indiana

All decorative art throughout this book is licensed through Canva and Canva Pro memberships.
Canva AI was used for art on pages 80, 81

Dedication

A dedication to the relentless souls committed to growth—we ascend the loftiest peaks in pursuit of the finest rewards. With steadfast resolve, we navigate one thing and one day at a time, recognizing that our most profound impact on growth stems from concentrating on what truly matters. In this journey, we discern that not all things are created equal, and through focused intention, we unearth the essence of meaningful progress.

Foreword

DMTakeshi ventures into the depths of hard-hitting subjects like depression and anxiety, offering readers a poignant insight into the author's emotional journey as she navigates the terrain of her inner world. Through a compelling blend of rapid-fire verses and poignant imagery within her collection of poems, DMTakeshi's words paint a vivid tale of resilience and introspection, guiding readers through the labyrinth of human emotions with amazing sensitivity. From the shadows of despair to the light of perseverance, each poem encapsulates an exploration of the delicate balance between pain and healing. With a deft touch, the author leads us on a transformative odyssey, transcending early traumas to unbreakable fortitude. "Readable/Unreadable" is not just a book of poetry; it is a profound reflection on the human experience.

This collection captivates with its raw honesty, inviting readers to immerse themselves in the author's world and emerge with a newfound appreciation for the resilience of the human spirit. With every turn of the page, DMTakeshi weaves a narrative that lingers in the mind, beckoning readers to return time and time again, each reading a new discovery in between the folds of her words and heartfelt emotions.

-Sara and Billie J

Author's Note

"Knowing yourself is the beginning of all wisdom"
– Aristotle

I extend a heartfelt invitation to readers, urging them to embark on a literary odyssey through the diverse landscapes of my emotional and existential journey. Within these pages, a narrative unfolds; woven with threads of joy, resilience, and the relentless pursuit of happiness. The collection is more than a compilation of verses; it is a chronicle of transformation, proof of my indomitable spirit's ability to transcend the shadows of despair.

My poetry delves into the complexities of self-discovery, resilience, and happiness. With every stanza; readers are invited to witness the transformation from "UNREADABLE," a metamorphosis from the cocoon of despair into the wings of joy. The collection serves; as a tribute to the transformative power of words and the commitment to seek happiness, even in the face of adversity.

As we traverse the corridors of this anthology, each stanza reveals a layer of self-discovery. The ink on the pages mirrors the nuanced hues of my experiences, each word a brushstroke painting the canvas of life. This journey unfolds from the abyss of despondency to the radiance of joy, an intricate dance of emotions that reiterates the symphony of existence.

In the heart of this collection lies a commitment; to celebrate the joy found in the intricacies of life, to acknowledge the struggles and triumphs, and to tell a story that resonates with the human spirit. As we embark on this literary voyage; may the words within "READABLE" serves not only as an expression of my journey, but as an invitation for readers to explore the depths of their own emotions—and to find solace, inspiration, and above all, happiness, within the pages of this collection.

Table of Contents

Author 2

Good Pen 4

No 6

Change In Me 8

Inner Peace 10

How Will You Remember Me? 12

When I'm All Alone Haikus 14

Gaia 16

Happy Things 18

Happiness Happens Within 20

I Forgot to Say 24

Manifesting Myself 26

Once Upon a Rhyme 28

Ketamine 30

Magically Mushedrooms 32

Enter Me Intravenously 34

You Are My Muse 36

Untitled 38

You Are Worth It 40

Self-Love 42

Creative Minds 44

Aeralyn 46

Cri 48

Crimson 50

Jellybean Jar 52

Starry Night 54

The Other Side of the Coin 56

Constructed Pleasures 58

Ashes of Technicolor Bruises 60

Angels Walked 62

Elusive Dancer 64

Growing Marigolds 66

Forbearance Haikus 68

Friendship 70

Home 72

How 74

I Just Want Coffee 76

Orion's Belt 78

Split Personality 80

There for You 82

messages from DiMension eighT 84

READABLE
Poetry and Prose

DMTAKESHI

Author

"Poetry is when an emotion has found its thought and the thought has found words." – Robert Frost

Keep your thesaurus close
and your pen closer,
the words will just flow
over and over.

Once a day—
start with nothing.
Once a day—
write something.

Sometimes it will suck.
Sometimes it will be profound.
Sometimes we won't give a fuck.
Sometimes we'll want to be crowned.

Commit to yourself
like you would your career;
every day you show up
and get into gear.

When you keep your thesaurus close,
and your pen even closer,
who knows?
Maybe one day you'll be an author.

A Bit About: Author

Author serves as a rallying call to the aspiring wordsmith, inviting them to embrace the creative journey armed with a thesaurus and a faithful pen. I am urging the reader to let the words flow effortlessly, a cascade of expressions that unfold "over and over." It is a spirited ode to the daily grind of writing, a celebration of both the process and the potential for growth and achievement in the world of words.

DM Takeshi

Good Pen

*"I don't care if a reader hates one of my stories,
just as long as he finishes the book" – Roald Dahl"*

I need a good book,
or better yet a good pen.
Don't overlook,
let's get back in again.

Haven't been here in so long—
it's just like riding your bike.
What could really go wrong?
What's there to dislike?

I've put it off for long enough,
I don't know why I stop
something that I claim to love—
but have many times just dropped.

It's like speaking my own language
that only I understand.
Like unraveling a package,
witnessing it firsthand.

I never know where I might conclude,
or from where I began…
and to be honest I surprise myself
to see just how the ink ran.

This one has been fun
to see where things may lead.
But all good things end,
even things—well-penned.

A Bit About: Good Pen

This unfurls the tale of my hiatus from the world of verse, a departure from the rhythmic dance of words. Yet, like an essential breath, poetry beckons me back. Its return is not just a resumption but a reconnection, an intrinsic and vital part of my existence that flows effortlessly, like a natural and necessary rhythm.

DM Takeshi

"When I dare to be powerful, to use my strength in the service of my vision, then it becomes less and less important whether I am afraid." – Audre Lorde

In this dance of affirmations, I've often nodded "yes."
Yet, for my well-being, a different course; I must confess.
No longer shackled by the chains of expectation,
I've embraced the might of "no," a newfound salvation.

No shadows of doubt now cloak my decisions in haze—
a liberation that colors my spirit in vibrant blaze.
Against your pressure, my resilience remains unwavering;
practicing clarity, I navigate without changing.

No longer swayed by the art of your persuasion,
I've unearthed a steadfast determination.
Your insistence—a force that shall implore no more,
for with unyielding certainty, "no" I now restore.

You may not coerce me to echo that word.
"No" resounds boldly, a voice finally heard.
Disregarding the times when it cast me low,
I've found strength in refusal, self-love to bestow.

Today marks the commencement of my decree
to stand up for myself, to express my liberty.
If you wish to remain, I must speak freely,
for in my newfound voice,
"No" is my choice.

A Bit About: No

A Bit About No is a declaration of empowerment and self-affirmation. It revolves around the decision to prioritize my well-being by embracing the power of saying "no." The verses convey a sense of liberation from the pressures of obligation and external expectations. I am reflecting on the past instances where I felt compelled to say "yes" despite the toll it took on my mental and emotional state.

Now, with newfound clarity and determination, I assert my right to decline and set boundaries. The poem captures a moment of personal growth, self-discovery, and the courage to stand up for oneself. It emphasizes the importance of choosing self-care and finding strength in the ability to assert one's own voice and boundaries.

DM Takeshi

Change In Me

"In any given moment we have two options: to step forward into growth or step back into safety." – Abraham Maslow

Feeling too good in my life
to notice the bad.
I'm enjoying the ride—
no longer so sad.

People all notice the change in me,
they see me for who I want to be.
This time feels so different,
I'm no longer belligerent.

My eyes are open
I see things in a new light.
I don't want to be broken.
I have a new sense of pride.

Breaking cycles.
Setting examples.
I'm racing to the finals
from the shambles.

My new outlook gives me passion.
I'm ready to take action.

A Bit About: Change In Me

Encapsulating a positive transformation in my life, this poem highlights a shift from sadness to joy. The change is not only visible to others but is deeply felt by me. I no longer identify with my past. I'm expressing a newfound sense of pride, openness, and passion, emphasizing a break from destructive cycles and a commitment to setting positive examples; radiating a sense of optimism and readiness to take proactive steps toward a brighter future.

Inner Peace

"Peace is not merely a distant goal, but the journey we embark upon within ourselves, a tranquil exploration of the soul." – Dalai Lama

*Finding that inner peace
instead of always trying to appease.
Protecting my precious energy
imprinted in my memory.*

*Calming down...
Eventually...
Intentionally...
Exceptionally...*

*Protect your own energy
and slowly download.
The mystery of the great synergy
upon which peace is bestowed.*

*When my anxieties arise,
I close my eyes.
While counting my breath—
I cease the threat.*

*Preserving my vigor
because I'm important.
My skin is thicker,
I'm no longer dormant.*

*I'm picking up my pieces,
peace by peace—
it's never out of reach.
My self confidence increases.*

A Bit About: Inner Peace

This poem is a journey toward inner peace, a conscious shift from constantly seeking external approval to prioritizing the preservation of one's precious energy. The pursuit of inner peace becomes an empowering journey, fostering increased self-confidence and resilience.

DM Takeshi

How Will You Remember Me?

"Legacy is not leaving something for people. It's leaving something in people."
– Peter Strople

I hope I was kind and caring,
I tried hard to understand.
I wasn't very daring,
but I hope I lent my hand.

I wasn't very courageous,
but I still desire your admiration.
May sound outrageous,
but I'd love to be someone's inspiration.

Inspiration to come from the dark
and overcome adversity.
Hopefully, I've left my mark
to the best of my ability.

Tomorrow is new,
so I'll keep trying
to become to a few—
a warrior climbing.

My destiny was once unclear,
but now I know why I'm here.

Readable

A Bit About: How Will You Remember Me?

In this poetic expression, I delve into the profound journey of leaving an indelible mark upon the world, a quest that intertwines with the discovery of my purpose. I articulate my personal triumphs over adversity, aspiring to embody a figure of inspiration for others to admire and emulate.

DM Takeshi

When I'm All Alone Haikus

"The only shame in masturbation is the shame of not doing it well."
– George Carlin

When I'm all alone,
I think of you often and
I want you to know.

    When I'm all alone,
    I touch myself in places
    that are left unknown.

        When I'm all alone,
        I'm longing for your soft touch
        I love you a bunch.

    Sometimes I touch me.
    Seems like I am on a throne—
    when I'm all alone.

When I'm all alone,
I touch my inner sanctum.
Yes, please! I condone.

A Bit About: When I'm All Alone Haikus

I crafted these haikus with the intention of unveiling a more sensual facet of my being. Embracing the beauty of self-discovery, I celebrate the art of masturbation, a profoundly intimate journey that not only enhances personal pleasure but also enriches the shared exploration with a partner. After all, isn't the essence of this experience rooted in understanding and reveling in our desires, thereby elevating the connection we share with ourselves and our beloved?

DM Takeshi

Gaia

"Put your ears to the ground, to the sky, to the sun and the moon... tune in to Mother Earth's sweet song. She has messages to say, knowledge to relay, inspiration to convey... there is much for you to learn. Your journey has just begun" – Melody Lee

Write the world a letter,
reach down to your center.
Show her your appreciation
for our idiosyncratic creation.

A promise to enhance,
and give our children a chance
to enjoy the worldly goddess.
We shall be more conscious.

Give her a glowing message—
we will heal the wreckage.
The brand new possibility
of giving—to our best ability.

With every breath I take
I feel the connection,
and sometimes the ache.
She pleads for our attention.

Close your eyes to revel in the view,
let her know what she means to you.

A Bit About: Gaia

This ode is a tribute to Mother Earth, celebrating her boundless wisdom, love, and innate generosity. In its verses, a gentle call resonates—to extend kindness not only to our planet but also to one another, acknowledging the interconnected harmony that weaves through the fabric of existence.

Happy Things

"Rare as is true love, true friendship is rarer." – Jean de La Fontaine

I want to write about happy things.
I want it to be a standard.
I want to write about the joy it brings.
I want to know it all mattered.

I hope to embark on new journeys,
because I want to grow.
Now in my late thirties,
I will work harder though.

My mind used to be toxic...
now I feel bubbly.
Contentment remains chronic,
I wish to do this humbly.

I'll move the stars,
then rearrange them just for you.
Grab our guitars,
then play them on cue.

Just for tonight we sit upright
while we hold each others hands,
the starry night will provide
us our simple commands.

So, when I say I want to write about happy things
you will know I mean you.
Pulling at my heartstrings
others will always misconstrue.

I want to write about happy thoughts—
we can both connect the dots.

A Bit About: Happy Things

I embarked on a journey intending to capture the essence of happiness. Yet, as the verses unfolded, they metamorphosed into a declaration of love—an eloquent truth to the profound affection I harbor for my husband and the unbridled joy he bestows upon me.

DM Takeshi

Happiness Happens Within

"Very little is needed to make a happy life; it is all within yourself, in your way of thinking." – Marcus Aurelius

What if we don't even know
where to begin,
and how will I know it
if I've never been?

Take my hand
right this way.
Nothing planned—
Make your day!

Screech!
Halt!
I can't reach—
It's not my fault.

Just one thing;
Let me amaze—
To you I'll bring
happier days.

Readable

The promise sounds too good
except for the impossibility.
Honestly, I wish I could,
but that would require stability.

Here's just one little secret,
take it with you as news;
happiness is needed—
and there when you choose.

I choose it.
Make me happy.
This is shit.
Make it snappy!

Feeling as though I cannot wait,
I am only told I must have faith.
How much longer can I last
before happiness has passed?

Don't stray.
Not too far.
It's right this way.
Save it for another day.
I'm tired and useless.
This life is ruthless.

DMTakeshi

Here's your gift,
arriving today—
you've never truly lived
and now, you'll stay.

I wouldn't believe you,
except I'm changed.
It was in me all along,
perfectly arranged

Does this moment give you peace?
Yes, I'll never leave.

A Bit About: Happiness Happens Within

At the inception of my quest for happiness, my pen reflected the yearning within me, a longing born from a lack of genuine encounters with joy. Now, with pride, I declare that through arduous self- discovery and determination, I have ventured inward, unearthing the elusive treasure of true happiness.

DMTakeshi

I Forgot to Say

"Friends are like stars; you may not always see them, but you know they're always there." – Christy Evans

Renee,

You helped me grow into the person I am today.
You gave me a voice and taught me how to use it;
to stand up for me and all my peeps.
You showed me the way,
and I'm grateful for you every single day.

Thank you, Renee.

A Bit About: I Forgot to Say

This is my ode to an extraordinary friend, a guiding light who bestowed upon me the invaluable lessons of embracing authenticity, standing resilient against any diminishing narratives, embodying courage, and fiercely safeguarding those you hold dear. I love you always, friend.

Manifesting Myself

"Your thoughts become things; manifest wisely." – Mike Dooley

My manifestation provides new sensations.
This guide, comprised of new heights;
exceeding all my expectations.
My old life no longer suffices.

With fine tuned precision
and actions to maneuver;
to life, comes our vision—
we are the producers.

To believe it is visualization;
seeing it through your imagination,
leading us to the synchronization
of the curious—with fascination.

I'm grateful for my preceding years
but that's no longer good enough.
Since my anxieties have disappeared,
I have turned to self-love.

A Bit About: Manifesting Myself

This stream of verses serves as a tribute to the transformative power of my manifestations, illuminating how they have steered my life toward greater tranquility. The reverberating of my past life, once familiar, now seem mismatched with the serenity I've discovered. As I journey forward, I am steadfast in my commitment to personal growth, continuously striving to evolve into a better version of myself through the practice of manifestation.

DM Takeshi

Once Upon a Rhyme

"We're all a little weird, and life's a little weird. And when we find someone whose weirdness is compatible with ours, we join up with them and fall in mutual weirdness and call it LOVE." – Dr. Seuss

Looking back in time,
I remember how we met
and now it seems like—
oh, so forever ago.
I was not too hard to get.
We were talking on the phone,
and we said, "Hello."

About us, I still wasn't sure,
so, I proceeded with caution.
Then, I learned
your heart was pure—
by then,
I was gotten.

While you didn't
"have me at hello,"
I was curious to learn
more about you.
Baby, you somehow won me over,
though,
because with me—
you stayed true.

...

People called it puppy love.

At fifteen,
they never would've believed we'd last,
but our love has remained tough
and in all this time we've created
a very strong past.

Remember when we felt
it was just a piece of paper?
So we waited a long time
before we were married.
I still remember how it felt—
so major...
those feelings were deeply buried.

Now we're older, gentler, finer
and we sometimes can forget,
but our love's a good reminder
of how we very first met.

Hello lover—
your presence
always
brings such color!

A Bit About: Once Upon a Rhyme

In this ode of love, penned with heartfelt gratitude, I celebrate the years shared with my husband, PJ. Our story commenced at the tender age of 15, and since then, an enduring love has blossomed and thrived. With each passing year, my appreciation deepens for the incredible journey we've undertaken together. PJ, you are not just a part of my life; you are my everything, and this love poem is evidence of the enduring bond we've cherished through the years.

Ketamine

"You can ask others for directions about your life's path... But remember, then you're on someone else's journey and may get lost. Search for your path within." – Nanette Mathews

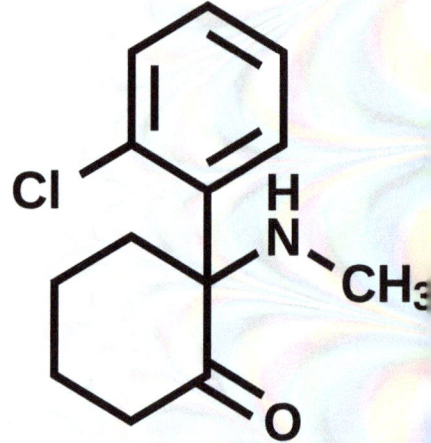

Bam!
160 milligrams
Straight to the dome
Returning home

Is all of everything the same?
Is this from where we came?
Here we go!
Overload!

Right where I'm supposed be
Fits perfectly
We are in sync
and on the brink...

The brink of breaking through
after the concoction is brewed
Dissociate to reflect
This is how I can connect

Now I know my purpose
It's come to the surface
Thank you, Ketamine
You've revealed what was unseen

A Bit About: Ketamine

Through the use of Ketamine therapy for my depression and anxiety, I was inspired to document parts of my journey through poetry, thus this piece emerged as a profound realization—a discovery of purpose that, until then, remained veiled in the depths of my being.

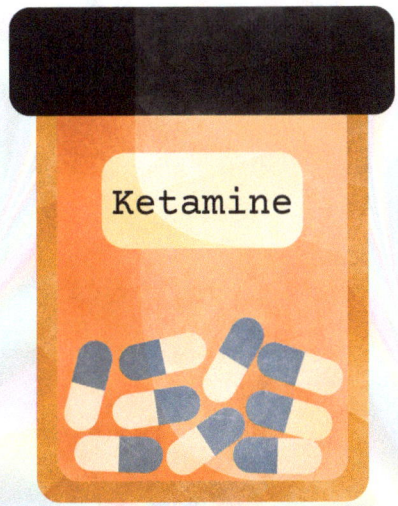
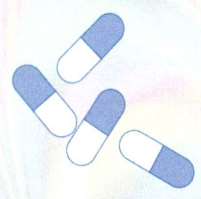

DM Takeshi

Magically Mushedrooms

"I see the mycelium as the Earth's natural Internet, a consciousness with which we might be able to communicate." – Paul Stamets

Magically they appeared
rooted in the ground,
so I volunteered
to learn something profound.

Ingested then digested
now we're going down,
time to be mended,
this is world-renowned!

Visions from the gods
and blanketed by warm feelings,
I like those odds—
and all of their teachings.

Next time you grow,
know where to go
so you can always flow
with the very best of pros.

*Mycelium equals freedom
when psilocybin gets eaten.*

A Bit About: Magically Mushedrooms

Born from my profound belief in the transformative potential of psychedelics, not merely as a means of healing but as a conduit for thriving, this piece came to life. Within the hallucinations, I find therapeutic landscapes that unfold realms of self-discovery, offering avenues to explore and embrace the intricacies of the human psyche. In the dance of altered perceptions, I see profound healing and growth, a journey where the mind not only mends but flourishes in its vibrant, kaleidoscopic expression.

DMTakeshi

Enter Me Intravenously

"Change the way you look at things and the things you look at change."
– Wayne W. Dyer

Lindsey sends me to outer space.
Tabor speeds up the pace.
The possibility of no responsibilities
as I slide into home base.

Hannah's there as well,
pushing me fast as a gazelle.
I will continue to learn
as I come to terms.

For I yearn to have the knowledge
that gives me confidence
with the privilege—
while it skyrockets.

Trying to find a good synonym
so I can keep plucking
away on my mandolin.

Enter me intravenously.
Passionately.
Casually.
And with certainty.

A Bit About: Enter Me Intravenously

This poem unfolds during my journey with Ketamine therapy, portraying the drug as a living embodiment of love. Beyond its chemical nature, this poetic narrative holds a profound revelation—Ketamine's intervention halted my suicidal thoughts with unshakable precision. Now, armed with newfound clarity, I embrace a deep desire to live a long, healthy life, transcending the shadows that once threatened my existence.

DM Takeshi

You Are My Muse

"The sky is love's muse." – *Walter Mercado*

For you, Valentine,
the day is meant to shine
for your personality, dramatically
advanced—past the glass ceiling, drastically.

You've turned a new leaf,
(I always knew you were impressive),
it's not hard to believe—
it's because you're effective.

Your electrifying nature;
you're intensifying greater.
So inspiring…
I need rewiring.

I won't hold you back;
you're an idol
for what I lack.
I'll make it vital.

Being attentive to my wants and needs
only looking forward,
onward,
full speed.

A Bit About: You Are My Muse

On Valentine's Day, I penned this poem for my husband, a tribute to the remarkable growth he has exhibited and the profound inspiration he has bestowed upon me. Witnessing his journey of self-improvement has kindled a sense of admiration that compels me to look up to him. Recognizing the strides he's made, I am resolute in my commitment not to impede his progress and, in the same breath, acknowledge the imperative need for my own transformation towards a better self.

DM Takeshi

Untitled

"One day I will find the right words, and they will be simple."
– Jack Kerouac, The Dharma Bums

Begin writing here...
Start with hands on the keyboard.
We just hope the message becomes clear—
and from our hearts, we poured.

But is anything *really* clear
or is the world mixed with grey?
Because I'm not sure if I fear
the words I try to convey.

Is that really what I wanted to admit?
I often think I can't commit
to my thoughts or words.
I'm not an influencer.

Just lost in this abyss
like a sunken ship.
Trained by society.
Full of anxiety.

I am also filled with hope—
and so much shame.
I have learned to cope
with writing on the brain.

Now we bring it to an end,
finishing touches, penned.

A Bit About: Untitled

My introspective poem provides a candid exploration of the complexities of self-expression and communication through writing. I grapple with the inherent uncertainty and ambiguity that often accompany the attempts to convey thoughts and emotions. There is a palpable sense of vulnerability and self-doubt as I question the clarity of my message.

Yet, amidst these challenges, there is a flicker of hope, and the act of writing becomes a therapeutic means of coping with the intricate interplay of emotions and navigating the tumultuous landscape of the mind. The poem concludes with a touch of finality, signaling the completion of the creative process and leaving the reader with a nuanced glimpse into my internal struggles and moments of resilience.

DM Takeshi

You Are Worth It

"When love runs soul deep, a kiss is no longer just a kiss. It is the place where heaven and earth meet." – Daniel Nielsen

In the tapestry of twilight
where stars softly gleam,
I found my forever
in the realms of a dream.

Through the dance of moments—
hand in hand,
we waltz on stardust,
in a love so grand.

Your touch—a sonnet
on my skin, it weaves
a melody of passion
that swears to never leave.

With every heartbeat,
a promise so true.
Forever entwined,
just me and you.

Your eyes like constellations,
deep and divine.
In their gaze is love's poetry—
an eternal line.

Through the seasons of life,
a love that stays.
An eternal sonnet
in our endless days.

So here's to us
in this cosmic embrace.
In the galaxy of love
you're my guiding grace.

Your touch imprinted
in our love's design.
A masterpiece of romance—
forever mine.

A Bit About: You Are Worth It

You Are Worth It is another poem for my loving husband in which I strive to capture the essence of his extraordinary nature—one that is truly unparalleled. Words falter in conveying the depth of my love and gratitude towards him, for he has stood steadfast by my side during the darkest hours. Now, poised to reciprocate the support, I am prepared to offer him not just my best, but the very essence of my being.

DM Takeshi

Self-Love

"Always remember, your focus determines your reality." – George Lucas

I recognize and am self-aware
and desire more action,
but I always seem to compare,
then I lose my traction.

From my affirmations
I want to be better, to do better.
I have aspirations,
but I let my anxiety fester.

Good for me for having dreams!
Let the toxic thoughts fizzle…
Get out all of your screams,
fine-tune happiness with a chisel.

One thing at a time.

This composition emerged from a wellspring of self-love and a commitment to self-care. In a conscious decision to break free from the shackles of sadness and neglect, I penned these verses as a testament to my newfound dedication to personal well-being.

The culmination of this piece carries a reminder—choosing the path of mindfulness and focusing on one thing at a time. It is a gentle encouragement to prioritize oneself, recognizing that genuine self-focus lays the foundation for everything else to fall into place.

DM Takeshi

Creative Minds

"You use a glass mirror to see your face. You use works of art to see your soul." – George Bernard Shaw

My proclivity for creativity
has produced me many riches,
brought me out of captivity—
removed all of my stitches

Healing through intimate anthologies,
kneading out the bleeding notions.
Gaining pristine intricate qualities
like majestic waves on the oceans.

Inking my *thinkings* more emphatically.
Systematically.
Dramatically.
Automatically.

Creative intellects
paving uncharted land—
are master architects
at designing to expand.

Muses manufacture bazookas
so I may write soulfully.
Even when she reduces,
I get by copiously.

Don't let your candle burn out
local hopefuls soaring.
Open your hungry mouth—
faith in art is restoring.

A Bit About: Creative Minds

Creative Minds sums up the profound journey of my creative spirit, an innate inclination that has proven to be a source of abundant richness and liberation. This creative outlet has proven to be my sanctuary, a profound source of solace amid life's myriad challenges. Art, with its transformative essence, serves as a healing balm, granting others a glimpse into the depths of my soul.

DMTakeshi

Aeralyn

"Motherhood: All love begins and ends there." – Robert Browning

Hello earthlings!
Aeralyn is your new leader.
Bring your offerings,
she couldn't be any sweeter.

She is braver than most.
She excels above and beyond.
Her heart—freely exposed—
your only wish to correspond.

Aeralyn is off the charts!
She is destined for great things.
Funny, brave and smart—
always pulling at heartstrings.

As your momma,
I need for you to know—
this life is full of trauma
but my love for you just grows.

Aeralyn, my baby,
you've brought tremendous joy to my life—
and sometimes drove me crazy...
without you, I can't imagine I'd survive.

It's an honor to watch you blossom—
proud and so fulfilling.
Your zest for life is awesome
and most certainly is thrilling.

She is crushing all routines
spiked with a bit of adrenaline.
My love is bursting at the seams
For the one and only—

Aeralyn.

A Bit About: Aeralyn

In the radiant intricacies of existence, my daughter Aeralyn shines as a beacon of courage, steady confidence, and profound inspiration. This poem is a tribute to her exceptional leadership abilities, a monument to the awe-inspiring force she embodies. My love for her—my eternal baby—knows no bounds.

DM Takeshi

"I want to make a difference in the world by speaking out and spreading hopeful messages. I want to send the message of 'you are not alone and you are safe' to other transgender kids." – Rebekah Bruesehoff

This beautiful blue girl
wanted to be a yellow boy,
so he gave it a whirl—
hoping to bring him great joy.

Your family will support you through
no matter what you choose,
they taught you to be you—
reinvent yourself and never lose.

So this beautiful yellow boy
became fully yellow.
How did it destroy
your fellow fellow?

It didn't.
They're just fine.
A little resistant—
but they won't cross the line.

He goes by Cri.
It's short for Crimson.
He's a regular, cool guy—
you just have to listen.

Readable

A Bit About: Cri

In this poem, I delve into the tale of my transgender son's journey. Through the prism of love and understanding, the poem navigates the nuances of identity, acceptance, and the beauty of embracing one's true self. It is a lyrical celebration of individuality and displays the unbreakable bond between a parent and their child.

DM Takeshi

Crimson

"A mother's love for her child is like nothing else in the world. It knows no law, no pity; it dares all things and crushes down remorselessly all that stands in its path." – Agatha Christie

Dearest Crimson,
Where has the time gone?
You'll be a star, risen—
everyone drawn.

You've taken life by the horns
and can't slow down.
Everyday you transform
to wear that crown.

Stand tall, child,
don't let them make you feel small—
you are free and wild;
and they can only crawl.

Doing big things—
I see it in your future.
Spread those 6 ft wings
and everyone will need sutured.

I remember you as a baby
I've loved watching you grow;
especially lately—
your shine provides a glow.

Dearest young man,
I will love you forever;
that's my plan
doubting—never.

You stole my heart before you were born;
this I want you to always know.
I'll always adore my firstborn
and I promise it'll always show.

A Bit About: Crimson

Crimson possesses an irresistible allure that draws people in like a magnetic force. I hold a profound belief that he is destined for stardom, a celestial presence that eternally resides in my heart. The sentiment encapsulated in these lines reflects a genuine and enduring love that transcends the passage of time.

My affection for you, Cri, remains steadfast, always and forever.

DM Takeshi

Jellybean Jar

*"When you know yourself you are empowered.
When you accept yourself you are invincible."* – Tina Lifford

This jellybean jar is full.
Guess how many there are...
Hundreds? Thousands?
Pours out, and disbands.

Betcha didn't see that coming—
now it's considered something.
So why build-up
just to tear down—

when so severely damaged?
It's a miracle to have managed.
Often it must face demolition
with the rebuild put on exhibition.

It was never meant to be...
a jar full of jellybeans.
This grand jar was meant to encompass
something magical and wondrous.

Today, it simply holds a mirror.
It helps to see things a little clearer.
Revealing who you have become
was the greatest magic ever done.

A Bit About: Jellybean Jar

Jellybean Jar is a tribute to my son's remarkable journey of self-discovery and transition into the incredible person he is becoming. I take immense pride in his courage to live authentically. It's a reminder that transgender individuals, both children and adults, deserve to be heard and seen for the genuine, wonderful people they are.

DM Takeshi

Starry Night

"Keep your face always toward the sunshine, and shadows will fall behind you." – Walt Whitman

I see your future, it looks bright.
Your brilliance is my guiding light.
Stars glist'ning in the abyss of night.
Your influential blastoff—takes flight.

You've got this made, Miss Starry Night—
it's History you will rewrite.
Witnessing the very best sights.
Shooting star in the sky—you will rise.

Like the sun, you shine over us.
Your charisma—a plus, and thus,
you trust that we won't make a fuss
when you leave so much to discuss.

Making that wish upon that star—
best decision I've made thus far.
It's hard how high you've set the bar.
You're now on everyone's radar.

Don't ever look back, Alley Cat,
just know you are on the right path.

Readable

A Bit About: Starry Night

In the poem 'Starry Night,' dedicated to Aeralyn, paints a vibrant portrait of her journey and potential. Each verse sparkles with the promise and brilliance of a starry night sky, reflecting Aeralyn's resilience and determination. From the guiding light of her brilliance to the influential trajectory of her dreams, the poem celebrates her transformation from 'Alley Cat' to 'Starry Night.' It captures the essence of her journey, rewriting history with each step, and inspiring awe like a shooting star in the sky. Aeralyn shines bright, casting a charismatic glow that leaves an indelible mark on everyone she encounters. 'Starry Night' is a testament to her unwavering spirit and the limitless heights she is destined to achieve.

DM Takeshi

The Other Side of the Coin

"I'm not concerned with your liking or disliking me. All I ask is that you respect me as a human being." – Jackie Robinson "

Hear what they say when you're not in sight—
I won't stop trying to change their mind.
Truth is I'm not good at helping them see;
it's only because we look differently.

But fact is we all want the same thing;
a simple chance at the freedom ring.
How do I help prove your life matters—
when they haven't taken in all the factors?

They refuse to see the systematic breakdown
simply because their skin tone is not brown.
They scream "If only he wasn't in opposition!"
"He shouldn't have been in that position!"

How can one understand white privilege
when reflecting in their own image?
They don't see the other side of the coin—
flip it on them and they'd readily join.

Readable

A Bit About: The Other Side of the Coin

The Other Side of the Coin calls for a transformative change, encouraging individuals to turn the coin of perspective. This challenge invites us to embrace empathy that goes beyond mere self-reflection, urging us to acknowledge the intrinsic worth present in every human life.

DM Takeshi

Constructed Pleasures

"The only journey is the one within." – Rainer Maria Rilke

I appreciate taking care of my soul—
it only hurt in the beginning.
Satisfying fates led to feeling whole—
my spirit vibrantly grinning.

I worked so fucking hard on me—
work-turned-reward, intentionally.
Bounteous payout,
for my land's layout.

Finally breathing easily—
look at my glow,
and now I have the decency
to let it all—just go.

Readable

A Bit About: Constructed Pleasures

Constructed Pleasures reflects the challenging journey I have navigated to become the person I am today. It narrates the unwavering effort and steadfast dedication to self-improvement that have marked my journey. Through these verses, I aim to express that, despite any obstacles, I remain committed to overcoming self-doubt and continually advocating for my own growth and well-being.

DM Takeshi

Ashes of Technicolor Bruises

"Hope rises like a phoenix from the ashes of shattered dreams."
– S.A. Sachs

A vibrant phoenix resurrected,
pondering life after death—they sweated.

Fortunate, they say, I am,
but veracity is laid by the fractured dam.

With these ashes of technicolor bruises,
my words have never felt more ruthless.

This deity breaks free of her harrowing chains,
valor pulsates through her embellished veins.

Gifting me…
immortality.

One last wish I never made…

Well played, my liege
I am now tortured, besieged.

Readable

A Bit About: Ashes of Technicolor Bruises

I crafted these verses inspired by a prompt from my dear friend, the incredibly talented poetess, Sara J. Her creativity and poetic prowess served as a catalyst, guiding the words onto the page.

Angels Walked

"No, I never saw an angel, but it is irrelevant whether I saw one or not. I feel their presence around me." – Paulo Coelho

Angels walked
Beside me and
Carried me while I
Desperately needed them
Eagerly they got me through the
Flames and then they
Guided me
High above the lands
In the sky
Just when I thought that their
Kind
Love faded they
Made sure I would be comforted
Never again would I be alone
Opening their hearts to me with
Passion
Quietly and
Remarkably they
Stayed
They were
Untiring I saw their
Value that night
Whereas I had never before
Xeroxing their infinite love
Yearning and
Zestful for life

A Bit About: Angels Walked

I penned this vibrant acrostic poem following a meditative moment that stirred my senses. In the midst of serenity, an indescribable presence enveloped me, and an intuitive belief whispered that angels graced the space around.

DM Takeshi

Elusive Dancer

"I do not try to dance better than anyone else. I only try to dance better than myself." – Mikhail Baryshnikov

Dancing does for me
what drugs cannot achieve;
that's because the beat's beyond
what one can conceive.

Dancing leads me to places
I love to explore in my mind—
it touches all of the bases
allowing me to unwind.

You can't dance without music—
It's made to evoke emotion,
it is very therapeutic;
combined, it feels like an explosion!

Maybe I need it—to be whole,
maybe it's to help me stay sane...
All I know is it has soul—
and provides a willful gain.

To have rhythm and beats
that feel like thunder,
rocking your feet—
creating your own wonder.

Getting down with my very own touch
but you will not catch me—dancing that much.

A Bit About: Elusive Dancer

Dancing holds a special place in my heart, even if my moves don't quite match the rhythm—a charming self-admission, if I may say so. The sheer joy of swaying to the music compels me to move, letting the infectious groove of the melodies guide each step.

Growing Marigolds

"The marigold is still open-hearted, and its tiny red orbited mirrors reflect the sky and trees." – May Oliver

Step One - Sow the seed right into the ground, this proves to be easy this time around.

Step Two - Barely anything—you need bring; wait until the ground is warm in spring.

Step Three - Water when the soil becomes dry— this annual will out of the ground—pry.

Striking blooms giving throughout the seasons, spanning beauty across many regions.

The oranges, whites, yellows and burgundies leave me feeling these calming certainties.

With having glamorous and bewitching designs. causing summer to be redefined.

Marigolds come and go every year— always bringing intoxicating cheer.

A Bit About: Growing Marigolds

Crafting this piece has been a delightful endeavor. It offers a peek into a larger short story I have penned, revolving around a woman coping with the loss of her mother, who holds a deep fondness for marigolds. Immersed in this creative journey, I have gained a fresh appreciation and insight into the significance of these flowers.

Forbearance Haikus

"The practice of patience develops the art of appreciation."
— Dalai Lama

Routines are a must.
Set expectations for me.
Meditation. Peace.

Patience, my Darling,
there's no need to rush around,
give yourself a break.

A Bit About: Forbearance Haikus

These haikus delicately unfold to emphasize the significance of restraint and the art of patient self-control. They invite contemplation on the necessity of practicing tolerance, both towards oneself and the world, as fundamental pillars for fostering inner peace and zest.

DM Takeshi

Friendship

"A real friend is one who walks in when the rest of the world walks out."
– Walter Winchell

Strong bonds,
meant to last.
Kind response—
love, surpassed.

Friends are meant to be there
when in need.
This we share,
LOVE, indeed.

Hold my hand,
it's you I trust.
Our relationship, grand—
our love, a must.

You are here for me again.
Thank you, my dear friend.

A Bit About: Friendship

Genuine friendship is an uncommon gem, and within these lines, I sought to underscore the profound significance of simply being there for someone. It delves into the essence of the human experience, emphasizing the paramount importance of having someone who shows up, a presence that can make all the difference in the world.

DM Takeshi

Home

"The ache for home lives in all of us, the safe place where we can go as we are and not be questioned." – Maya Angelou

There's a place I love to visit;
in there, I rest with my soul,
it keeps me in good spirits,
while it also keeps me whole.

I breathe to release my tension,
close my eyes to help me focus;
thrown in another dimension—
and then I begin to notice.

Inside this place I make a home,
imbibe the offerings given,
then I will set out on my own,
until I finish my mission.

Allow my mind to wander a moment
before I go for concentration.
This is how I remain content—
it's my perfect combination.

My home provides an insight
to what should've been clear;
the message was sent on expedite,
so I could rehear.

My home assists me to see.
My home is inside of me.

A Bit About: Home

Within each of us lies the sanctuary of inner peace, patiently waiting for our return. Take a moment to journey back home to this tranquil core. Embrace the exploration, for in the pursuit, you may uncover profound greatness awaiting your discovery.

DM Takeshi

How

"Creativity is intelligence having fun." – Albert Einstein

HOW
THESE WORDS JUST FLOW OUT
SPEWED FROM THE MOUTH
VIBING WITH MY CLOUT

HOW
PROVE I DESERVE THE TITLE
TO BE ARTISTICALLY VITAL
I'VE MADE IT TO THE FINALS

HOW
IT IS TIME TO SPIT NOW
BEFORE SHIT GOES SOUTH
GIVE THEM NO DOUBT

HOW
PRESENT MY PIECES
TO SPEAK IN SPEECHES
KNOWING THE SPAN IT REACHES

HOW
INFLUENCE THE CHANGE
RESET AND REARRANGE
RETURN TO THE STAGE

HOW
I DO IT VERY WELL
CAST YOU UNDER MY SPELL
THESE WORDS I PROPEL

YOU ASK ME HOW
SO I TOOK A VOW
THE POWER OF THESE WORDS
WILL MOVE THIS EARTH

STRENGTH

HUMBLE

TRUST

VALUES

RESPECT

A Bit About: How

This poem conveys a powerful message about creative and expressive prowess. The repetition of the word "How" at the beginning of each stanza emphasizes the questioning and contemplation of the process of artistic expression. The closing lines are a strong commitment and belief in the transformative potential of words, pointing out a profound sense of purpose and impact. Overall, the poem explores the dynamic and influential nature of artistic expression and the determination to wield this power effectively.

DM Takeshi

I Just Want Coffee

"Adventure in life is good; consistency in coffee even better." – Justina Chen

My husband is making me write a poem—
forcing me so I can have coffee.
But, my poems are broken…
I feel it in my body.

I have writer's block happening,
it can happen from time to time.
Sometimes it is maddening,
and other times it may be a sign.

Slow down, Jenn.
Things will fall into place.
You might be asking, "When?"
But this is not a race.

My husband is right,
"Just write the words as a hobby."
I will not fight…
I just want coffee!

A Bit About: I Just Want Coffee

This tale is as genuine as they come! In a whimsical turn of events, my husband held the coveted coffee hostage until I wove a poem. The lighthearted coercion left me both amused and appreciative. Ah, the lengths love will go.

DM Takeshi

Orion's Belt

"We are all connected; To each other, biologically. To the earth, chemically. To the rest of the universe, atomically." – Neil deGrasse Tyson

A beautiful string of pearls
blanketing the night sky
in this hazardous world—
I'm reminded to reignite.

I can always find you,
and you keep an eye on me.
My dreams will help me pursue
so things come more easily.

I appreciate your guidance,
(as you know I am in need).
New possibilities on the horizon
for me to snatch up indeed.

The best things come in three.
Thanks for watching out for me.

Readable

A Bit About: Orion's Belt

In the vast celestial universe, Orion and his iconic belt stand as the singular constellation that I not only recognize but unfailingly locate. The familiarity I share with this stellar formation goes beyond mere astronomical awareness; it extends into the realm of a profound connection.

This connection transcends the boundaries and becomes a personal tether to the mysteries of the universe, anchoring me in a sense of cosmic belonging. Orion, with its radiant belt, becomes a symbolic guardian, a celestial companion that watches over me amidst the boundless beauty of the cosmos.

DM Takeshi

Split Personality

"If you have the ability to love, love yourself first." – Charles Bukowski

Because I didn't like myself,
I knew I needed help.

I just don't want to *like* me—
and you'll never hear me utter,
"I want to live."

The world is cold;
no one could convince me that
everything is okay.

I don't want love.

Why lie and say
I am content?

I know that
nothing is fine;
and I'll never believe
someone like me deserves love.

I'm not worthy.

I won't ever announce,
my love for me is pronounced.

My love for me is pronounced.

I won't ever announce,
'I'm not worthy.'

Someone like me deserves love,
and I'll never believe
nothing is fine.

I know that
I am content.

Why lie and say
I don't want love?

Everything is okay!

No one could convince me that
the world is cold.

I want to live!

And you'll never hear me utter,
"I just don't want to like me."

I knew I needed help—
because I didn't like myself.

A Bit About: Split_Personality

This reverse poem serves as a poignant reflection of the tumultuous emotions I grappled with before embarking on my transformative journey towards happiness, emerging from a state of self-hatred. Through the ingenious reversal of verses, it captures the profound shift from despair to self-affirmation, providing a vivid portrayal of the emotional terrain I navigated on my path to self-love and contentment.

DM Takeshi

There For You (Tanka)

"Being there for someone during their darkest times is the greatest testament to unconditional love." – Dodinsky

I want to be there
when you feel like you're broken—
for I'll always care
about the words you've spoken.

I want you to be open.

A Bit About: There For You (Tanka)

Tankas, a delightful form of poetry, offer a playful avenue for creative expression. In this particular piece, I tenderly express my profound affection and care for my cherished family and friends.

DM Takeshi

messages from DiMension eighT

"Psychedelics show you what's in and on your mind, those subconscious thoughts and feelings that are hidden, covered up, forgotten, out of sight, maybe even completely unexpected, but nevertheless imminently present."
– Rick Strassman

1,2,3 BLASTOFF!
SHOWING ME AROUND
AFTER THE TAKEOFF
LANDING ON UNCHARTED GROUND

SHOWN IN ALL DIRECTIONS
MUCH TO MISUNDERSTAND
WITH SO MANY QUESTIONS
WISDOM AND IGNORANCE GO HAND IN HAND

IF ONLY THIS BIRD COULD HEAR ME
SHE WOULD KNOW HOW SCARED I AM
BUT SHE OBVIOUSLY DOESN'T NEED
TO GIVE A SINGLE DAMN

DON'T BE FRIGHTENED
THE BIRD KINDLY WHISPERED
YOU'RE ABOUT TO BE ENLIGHTENED
AND SHE TOOK ME TO SEE THE LIZARD

THE WISE LIZARD TAUGHT ME SO MANY THINGS
BUT IT NOW SEEMS HAZY LIKE A DREAM
THE BIRD TOOK ME BACK ON HER WINGS
NOW IT'S SO CLEAR THAT I COULD SCREAM

PATIENCE MAKES US GOOD PEOPLE
AND KEEPS THE WORLD MORE PEACEFUL
QUIT TALKING SO MUCH
EMBRACE WITH SOFT TOUCH

DON'T FORGET TO HELP YOUR FELLOW HUMANS
WE NEED TO BE IN THIS TOGETHER
ALWAYS LOOK FOR THE MOST NOBLE SOLUTIONS
HALT THE SUPERCILIOUS OPPRESSORS

IT'S POSSIBLE TO LEAVE THINGS IN BETTER SHAPE
BETTER TO HAVE A BEAUTIFUL LANDSCAPE
YOU WILL WANT TO LOVE EACH OTHER MORE
THIS ONE YOU DO NOT WANT TO IGNORE

WHEN I LANDED SAFELY BACK AT HOME
I KNEW I WAS NOT ON MY OWN

A Bit About:
messages from DiMension eighT

This poetic tapestry woven from the threads of my personal metamorphosis,
a profound account that unfurls under the powerful influence of DMT—
a psychedelic journey that transcends the ordinary boundaries of consciousness.

Within the patterns of verses, I invite readers to travel the sacred realms where
perception goes beyond the mundane and steps into the extraordinary.
It's not just about the psychedelic experience; it's an exploration of the self,
a profound revelation of growth and transformation.

DM Takeshi

(c) 2024 Readable/Unreadable; A Poetry Collection
Author: DMTakeshi
Editor, Formatting, Artistic Design: Brandy Lane

All rights reserved.
Printed in the United States of America.

No part of this book may be used, stored in a system retrieval system,
or transmitted, in any form or any means—by electronic, mechanical, photocopying, recording, or reproduced in any manner whatsoever—without written permission from the author, except in the case of brief quotations embodied in critical articles and reviews.

Published in the United States of America by:
Where Beautiful Inks LLC
Fort Wayne, Indiana

ISBN: 978-1-7363268-9-3

Library of Congress Control Number:

All pictures throughout this book are available through Canva and Canva Pro.   *Canva*

DEDICATION

They won't get it.

PJ, Cri and Aeralyn. May our freak flags fly high. Always go against the grain and take those risks. Be proud to love the strange things that make your weird, little hearts happy.

author's Note

DMTakeshi really has no business writing a book of poems. There is certainly no good reason for you to want to read an adventurous poem book likely written by a disturbed person.

If you still decide that this may peak your interest, let me set the bar extremely low for you. DMTakeshi has zero credentials and these poems have a high probability that they are the ramblings of a person with a serious mental illness. Enjoy!

TABLE OF CONTENTS

Please Excuse 2

Premises, Premises 3

Twisted 4

Sober Without You 5

Done With The Shit Today 6

Divine Inspiration 7

Mystic Capacity 8

Interrupted 9

Per Aspera ad Astra 10

It's Nothing 11

Focus 12

Vulnerable 14

Conceive It 15

Dreamed Once Before 16

Forever Blooming 18

Hey Mary 19

Abstruse 20

Taking Music in the Rooms that DreaMT 22

Dreaming Minds Together 23

Too Advanced Too Suite 24

Tell Me the Labels that you Reject Too	25
Stupid	26
Whore	27
Skinny	28
Fat	29
Crazy	30
Weak	31
Ugly	32
Bitch	33
Now	34
Confined	35
Attenjenn Miss Unforjennate	36
Undecided	38
Fabrication	39
Psypher	40
Life Lessened	41
If Only I Could	42
An Entire Generation	43
Shackles	44
Tense Ever Since	45

Overly Judgmental 46

Invasion of Privacy 47

Always Paying 48

Zero Fucks 49

Delightful Opposition 50

I Have No Friends 51

Last Exhausted Breath 52

Please, and Thank You 53

Comfortable Troubles 54

Bon Voyage 55

Insignificant Being 56

Not Shooting for Better 57

Tick 58

Doom and Gloom 59

Ramblings of Me(ntal Illness) 60

Cyclical 61

I personally wouldn't read it

PoEMs

uNReaDaBLe

DMTakeShi

Some crazy lady's
book of poems

DMTakeshi

PLEASE EXCUSE

Please excuse—
my depressive demeanor,
for I don't choose—
what can linger...

So, please excuse—
my side that is lacking,
for IT has been misused—
without even asking!

Pretty please excuse—
the huge mess I've made.
I tried to diffuse—

but the bomb exploded, anyway.

pREMisis, pREMisis

Saw the sparkle in her eye—
so hopeful... and careless...
Made sure that played out to die
now disposable... and helpless...

Killed her dreams loudly—
for her I never vouched.
She no longer stands proudly—
just in the corner—crouched.

TWisTEd

My emotions pour in like a flood.
The cuts put it into perspective.
Creating art with the blood.
At best I am defective.

>I am nothing special.
>I have no fancy hat—or shoes.
>You don't have to settle...
>and I have nothing to prove.

>>We all root for a good loser
>>who can turn their life around...
>>they focus on their future—
>>the purpose they have found.

I can't be a sheep.
I continue to search for change.
I won't stay asleep.
I like to keep it strange.

Fuck that life!

>>Who will turn down that dial?
>>Who will change their tune?
>>Fuck that ish!
>>Let's get ready to consume.

People gushing to lay it out for you.
Everyone knows better and their word is true.

"Trust me and listen here."

I don't play by the rules or live in fear.

SobER WiThoUT you

Exasperated by the childish game.
Sober without your love.
Tense—and you're to blame.
Confused now that I'm above.
Frightened to be alone.
Trembling but I'll show you.

Your true side you have shown.
Easing your mind with what you knew.

Manipulation left no room for me.
Irritated by your show.
Blessed now that I am free.
Indulged now that you know.

DMTakeshi

DONE WiTh ThE ShiT ToDAY

I am sorry I didn't stand up to you sooner.
I left your party and your future.

You'll never be ready and we are all tired.
This shit is petty and I'm not required.

I'm done with this shit today, I am ready to fight back.
We are not your prey—I'm set to attack.

I'm done with your shit today, this was long overdue.
I wish it was yesterday... before your shittiness grew.

And I'm not done taking it out on you.
We have finally won! And it's all brand new.

The world seems so bright because you're not here.
This is not out of spite—it's without fear.

I'm done with this shit today, I will always fight back.
Won't let anyone fall to your prey—I will fucking attack!

I'm done with your shit today, and this was long overdue.
If only I could change yesterday, I'd simply say...

"FUCK YOU!"

DiViNE iNSpiRATioN

Must be divine inspiration—
qualities that make me fiend.
Unheard of temptation—
outrageously weak in the knees.

Such a curious nature—
blinded by the light.
Led me to the next level—
and gripped me with such might.

Sucked into the illusions—
and now the truth is out.
Come up with your own conclusions—
but I have no doubt.

MYSTIC CAPACITY

I used to see clearly and the dreams came easily,
but then; my eyes started hurting me.

Why would anyone want to know
which way the wind will blow?

I used to see. It was so very clearly...
For a young child it was too much.
"You may see, but you cannot touch."

Sometimes it would be amazing,
and always persuading...
my mind I was losing—
for it was fear I was choosing.

Now I try so hard to see—
SIGHT has left fleetingly.

My gift—due to depart.
I hope it has found another heart.

Unreadable

iNTERRupTEd

Sometimes we have a reason and a choice—
just not always our voice.
Follow the thought.
Finish the prayer.
By evening it's over—
and never any simpler.

DMTakeshi

PER aspERa Ad asTRa

Desires can torment the spirit,
you keep asking yourself, "Why?"
Fantasies take their toll—
but you know they'll never die.

Fighting is not easy,
but persistence is my mission.
Dreams married to misery—
if only they saw my vision.

My soul bleeds,
the target—clearly drawn.
My essence is broken,
but my ambitions live strong.

Surviving on blind faith—
and I'm starving for more.
My aspirations will not go to waste,
now that this is what I've prepared for.

PER aspERa Ad asTRa... aNd bEYoNd.

Unreadable

        What happens when you just...
                let things happen?

        Spending 20 hours on the tube.
Everyone in a separate room.

        Lost control, never gained a vision.

        Always questioning the good I'm doing.

    What am I ruining?
                Not committing.
        And therefore nothing happens.

    And I let it.

               Is that what I feel inside?
                        Nothing.
        Is that all I'll ever see or dream?
                      Is that me?
                        Nothing.
        Or is that all I'll ever be?
                    What's wrong?
                      It's Nothing.

DMTakeshi

Focus

At your very core—
what do you long for?

That inner being—
what is it seeing?

Deep down inside—
what is it that you hide?

Follow your dreams—
and your soul beams.

Unreadable

F ulfillment

O penness

C reativity

u nity

S elf-love

DMTakeshi

I fear writing my thoughts and dreams—
disheveled at the seams.
Misleading is my inner being—
violently colliding.

My desolate soul with those hindered.
Before I can commit to being saved,
I pray I am adequate—
leaving me exposed.

CONCEIVE IT

...But that world does
exist.
Is it so hard to
conceive.
Beautiful minds can come together;
amazing things to be—
achieved.
Our children's future is brighter,
close your eyes to see.
This world exists—
but only if we
believe.

We stamp out the violence.
Good riddance to the hate.
Let go with turbulence.
Push past the dark on faith.

It's not the way we were wired—
there's only one ending...
Implode.
We are crying to be cured.
Searching for relief.
Souls in need of saving.
Begging you to...
Believe.
Beautiful minds can come together—
this is how we are all connected.
Human deeds for human needs.

DMTakeshi

dReaMt oNcE BEFoRe

I dreamt once before—
BUT the whole world LIED to me.
I will not try anymore.
I accepted them all to some degree.

I used to pray—
BUT I don't see the point.
The world just gets in the way,
and I wouldn't want to disappoint.

Nothing is going to change,
and I no longer believe—
YET I find it strange,
I was so easily deceived.

So I dreamt once before—
BUT I no longer can anymore.
I fell really hard,
I won't let down my guard.

No one can hear my screams.
Furious from the deception.
Giving up on all dreams—
there is no exception.

Unreadable

I just hide my face.
It's full of disgrace.
It's full of shame.
And I'm to blame.

I can't face the world.
Ignorance stole my bliss.
My body begins to curl.
Ending it with a deadly kiss.

People wonder what happened
to the flame I once had in me.
It's all because the whole world lied.

And I believed.
And I dreamed.
BUT nothing was ever going to change.

DMTakeshi

FoREveR BLooMiNG

Stunning moments, so curiously captured—
is that all that has ever mattered?

Dancing melody, infinitely looping,
eagerly enhancing, and forever blooming.

I'm entrusted to this alluring repeat—
deliberately chosen to sow this seed.

Trembling; to master my execution.
The hunger to inspire this evolution.

All possibilities, crossed by fulfillment—
implemented with every commitment.

These won't be remembered as the good ol' days—
stay consistent and persevere to amaze.

Those are sworn into your future endeavors,
labors; rewarded with the finest nectars.

Mighty urges hypnotize all that you see—
pining for the takeover passionately.

Dancing melody infinitely looping,
eagerly enhancing, and forever blooming.

Depended on—by many.
But I was untiring—I know I'm ready.

HEY MARY

With your eyes so green,
scorching with a blazing ember;
I really must come clean—
this I want us to remember.

Very seductively endowed,
but you make me ache for more.
You leave me in such a cloud,
impatient for what's in store.

I'm your trusted devotee,
a smile kept upon my face.
For that's your guarantee,
and it's never out of place.

I don't want you off my mind—
your high soothes my dalliance.
Potent and bewitching design—
strokes with enchanting ambience.

DMTakeshi

abstRusE

You may not know...
I am a proud mother
of two amazing human beings.
I'm also a passionate lover.
My tribe always bringing new teachings.

You may not know,
but here goes...

I am often full of anxiety,
but also extreme love.
I like me, finally,
but not nearly enough.

I am thirty-four
and have no direction.
It's becoming hard to ignore—
weighted by my imperfections.

I'm grateful for all I've underwent,
but damn it, I am aging terribly.
Not how I saw my life being spent—
ultimately, recovering mentally.

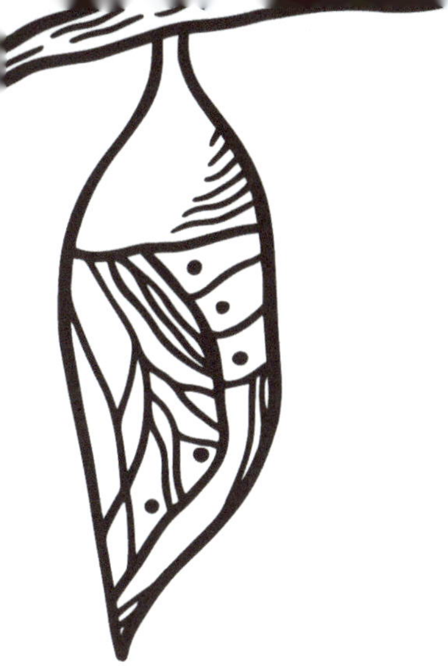

Unreadable

You may not know.
I'll show you though...

I'm really fucking strong,
with no follow through—
many struggles lifelong,
but never misconstrue.

I am loyal and devoted,
reliable and timely.
My heart has eroded—
jaded, but only slightly.

If I had to define me;
I'd like for you to understand—
I wish I tried harder
to show you who I am.

You may not know,
who I am really—
but I'd like to grow,
presenting me fiercely.

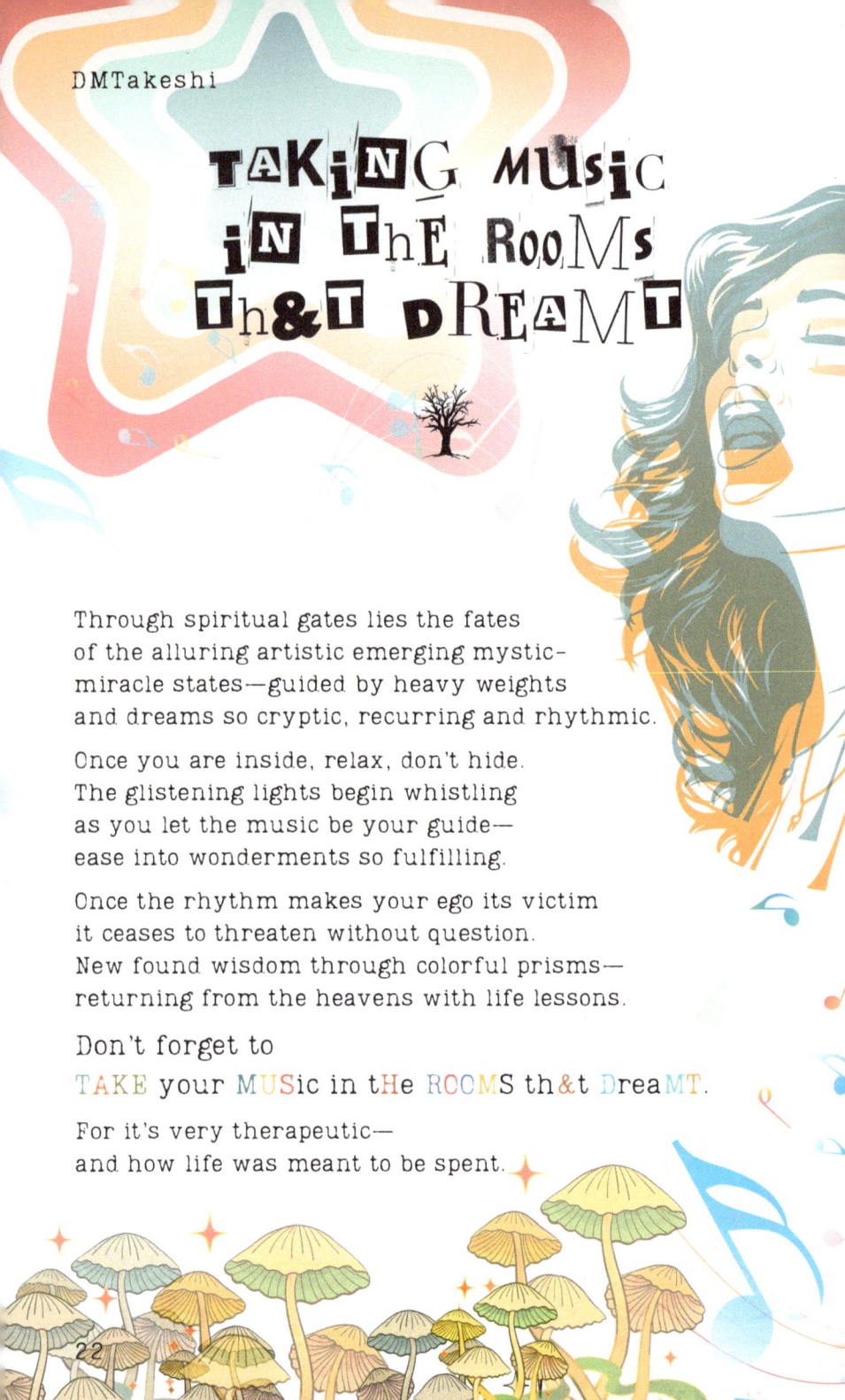

DMTakeshi

TAKiNG MUSic iN ThE RooMs Th&T dREaMT

Through spiritual gates lies the fates
of the alluring artistic emerging mystic-
miracle states—guided by heavy weights
and dreams so cryptic, recurring and rhythmic.

Once you are inside, relax, don't hide.
The glistening lights begin whistling
as you let the music be your guide—
ease into wonderments so fulfilling.

Once the rhythm makes your ego its victim
it ceases to threaten without question.
New found wisdom through colorful prisms—
returning from the heavens with life lessons.

Don't forget to
TAKE your MUSic in tHe ROOMS th&t DreaMT.

For it's very therapeutic—
and how life was meant to be spent.

DREAMING MINDS TOGETHER

Our bodies are possessed—
vividly glowing veins.
We were suppressed—
now we go through the change.

Ability to see every molecule—
our bodies intertwined.
Life without ridicule—
Baby, you were hard to find.

Discovering connections
as I feel them from inside—
and it's just as I suspected,
we harmonize to coincide.

Nature can take us there;
returning to world peace.
Dreaming minds, together;
it's our fears we must release.

TOO AdVaNCEd TOO SUiTE

Just when you thought that it had ended—
the story actually commences.
Life, as it was intended—
delivers your promised successes.

Past afflictions erased—
you are Earth's galaxy.
It's your time, it's your place.
You're the SUITE treasure found in tragedy.

Just when you couldn't see your greatness,
and it became all too much;
overnight you became famous—
you once envisioned it as such.

Your obsessions provided bounteously;
passion bled through these masterpieces.
on that ADVANCED level frequency—
leaving the whole world speechless.

DMTakeshi

S everal slanders suited.

T ake your pick.

U nderstandably wounded.

P ieced back together quick.

I gnorance disguised as bliss.

D etrimental remarks can't be dismissed.

Unreadable

W atchful minds so selective.

H umans always judging.

O r is it just perspective?

R emembering someone's something.

e ven though you can't really know.

DMTakeshi

S ometimes stars long to shine.

K now it's fine if they're grey.

i mpressive has left its sign—

N ot on me I'm afraid.

N ow let us move onward.

y esterday was torture.

Fortunately, I'm okay,

as a friend has set me free—

Told me today that I looked pretty.

DMTakeshi

Carefully selecting my battles,

Regardful of what's worn on my sleeve.

a nyone can see the scandals—

z anily trying to achieve.

y esterday's wants turned future shackles.

Unreadable

Wondering why we continue

even though we are broken.

assistance was never the issue—

Kindness viciously stolen.

DMTakeshi

U niquely made.

G rotesquely dismayed.

L onely in this notion.

y our emotions cautiously chosen.

Unreadable

But nothing hurts more with these

i ssues lying deep

T han the words that pour from

C lean hands turned cheap.

H ow have you risen above?

DMTakeshi

NoW

I'm too old to be playing
on someone else's terms.
I'm ready to start slaying—
I hope it really burns.

This is for me.
This is for family.
This I do happily—
and that pays out handsomely.

I won't worry about that deadline.
I create my own lifeline.
Still, I have no guideline.
Just no longer silent on the sideline.

I drink my own juice.
I dance when I cry.
I will let loose.
I no longer comply.

When I die—
I will say that I've lived.
I don't have much, but
my time is a precious gift.

#

I'm not the person you remember.
Everyone recalls me differently.
Reminiscing of past endeavors—
I am treated with such dignity.

      If you think I'm so fucking cool—
      then why didn't you show it?
      I think you've interchanged kind and cruel—
      sadly, you'd never know it.

           Why do you have this picturesque vision?
           Our flaws bring out our humanness.
           Making me perfect leaves me imprisoned
           to be the light to your luminous.

In all honesty,
you were never ready.
For this kind of quality—
and so you're left empty.

           Because you have this delusion
           that when you left things, remained.
           You've created an illusion—
           that cannot be explained.

      "You were the best I've had."
      You tell me all the time.
      It just makes me look sad.
      How was I so sublime?

If I am so sublime,
why are we no longer a team?
It leaves me to be confined—
as *the girl of your dreams.*

DMTakeshi

aTTENJENN Miss uNFoRJENNATE

HER JENNERIC HOT URJENNCY
JENNTLE BUT INADVERTENTLY

JENNITALS RENDERING A DREAM
GET THE ENJENNS READY TO STEAM

YOUR DIVERJENNCE CREATES A SKEPTIC
BITCH IS HYPOALLERJENNIC

MY JENNDER IS TASTY AND TENDER
JENNUINE CRAVING FOR THIS TASTE
JENNTRIFIED AND LEFT DISPLACED

JENNERATION DESPERATION
YOU'RE DUMB FUCKING WITH JENNOCIDE
JENNERATING YOUR SUICIDE

INTELLEJENNCE PAIRED WITH DILIJENNCE
DON'T JUDGE HER FOR HER NEGLIJENNCE

HER TANJENNTS ARE LEJENNDARY
VERY STRINJENNT ABOUT HER MARY

JENNERALIZING JUST A SMIDJENN
JENNETICALLY SHE CAN HAVE CHILDREN
BUT FILLED WITH TOO MANY CARCINOJENNS
AND THE OXYJENN POISONED BY ITS CITIZENS

HERE'S THE STATEMENT FROM HER AJENNT
WHAT HAPPENS WHEN YOU IMAJENN
REJENNERATION PUT IN ACTION

UNDER THE CONTINJENNCY
THAT THIS IS THE BIGGEST EMERJENNCY

AND WHILE WE APPRECIATE THE INJENNUITY
YOUR INDULJENNCE IS NOW UNDER SCRUTINY

WHAT HAPPENED IN JENNESIS
GAVE BIRTH TO DIVULJENNCE
AND HYDROJENN—ITS EMPHASIS
WHILE THE AJENNDA SHED ITS INNOCENCE

DMTakeshi

My future has always made me sick.
Knowledge bestowed is a privilege.
Choosing destiny feels like a trick!

My visions reveal a blank message.

When will it be enough?
When will I measure up?

When your failure still lingers...
and won't motivate the free thinkers.

The withdraws cause flaws to snarl their jaws—
and tomorrow needs to borrow your sorrow.

The gravity of this profanity leads to insanity—
and damn it all if this hasn't made me feel small.

I won't ever be the same,
but hopefully tomorrow, there lies change.

Unreadable

FaBRiCaTioN

Sexy in your deceitful nature.
Misleading your whole way through.
Provoked fraudulence in your future.
Dishonest because that's all you knew.

Cautious when you took that oath.
Very particular about what was said.
Obvious when you slit our growth.
It's all-too-familiar when your heart is dead.

Deception can be tricky.
But I'm uncomforted if it's true.
Verisimilitude makes me giddy.
Because I know it's dishonest coming from you.

DMTakeshi

0-0-1-0.
He is a goddamn hero.
Let us desire to unveil.
Psypher presides over this hell.
Psypher decides our rights.
Put our trust in this system.
It has been a mirage of fights.
We won't play the sad victim.
Lay bare the brute wicked truth.
Brings to light the enigma to you.
Psypher's tongue will softly soothe.
Colluded to recruit few.
The few that remain elite.
The chosen doomed to defeat.
Encryption through invading.
Algorithms always changing.
0-0-1-0.
Where is your fucking hero?

LiFE LEssENEd

It really doesn't fucking matter
if you're kind, or nice, or loving.
The world won't let that be a factor,
and in turn, will provide you with nothing.

You will always be second class,
because you won't stomp on their backs.
If you hope to surpass,
then be a dick—to the max.

They don't deserve you.
You're too good for this place.
Run! Don't misconstrue.
Go on! Get out! Escape!

Even people perceived as kind—
suck—and we're all blind.
You're the only one!!
Go on, get out! RUN!!

DMTakeshi

iF ONLY i CoULd

Awaken from this reality...
Not cause so much hurt...
Cease obnoxiously taunting me...
Wipe my face of this dirt...
Escape from me...
Exchange my life for a deserving birth...
Exit this society...
Distinctly show you your own worth...

An Entire Generation

An entire generation—
just wanting to off themselves.
Please, help their desperation;
while guns rest upon shelves.

We are deprived of all connection;
objects before people.
Innocent games turned obsession—
not all times, created equal.

Where do we go from this point?
Where do we stand?
Forced to disjoint.
Coerced to disband.

Eliminate all authority
and their virtuous malevolence.
The need to lose conformity
has never been so evident.

What if we broke the norm;
didn't pay those bills,
refused to perform—
indulged in the thrills?

An entire generation
actually savoring their time,
before their expiration—
shouldn't be such a vile crime.

DMTakeshi

#

My shackles began to bruise,
distress depleting my soul.
Working with a short fuse,
lost my head and control.

Better now that we're released,
my muscles couldn't remember another.
Self-worth increased,
and confidence—uncovered.

You thought we couldn't make it,
you thought we needed you—
truth was we were done faking it.
Did you fully think it through?

Justifying reasons,
feeding your sophomaniac.
What about your demons?
Wicked secrets about to crack.

Increasing and impeding deception.
Controlling through manipulation.
Always imparting your impression.
Requiring you causes debilitation.

Unreadable

TENSE EVER SINCE

Seeking the answers to tough questions
often serves you a very harsh truth.
Leaving you with these newfound tensions,
investigating your current route.

You desperately sought change,
but now you understand why
it must all remain the same—
destiny simply implied.

Beside you lies this comfort;
yet it's so far out of reach.
Instead, you're meant to suffer—
rest in joy—and you're in breach.

Did you really need to know?
Already so lost and broke.
Stunted life led to hindered growth.
Truth sought out to be evoked.

I've been so tense ever since.

DMTakeshi

OVERLY JUdGMENTAL

Piercing words disguised
as being friendly...
covertly detrimental.
Unsolicited advice is so empty.

Worry about your own disaster.
Your life is looking lonely.
You're no longer the ringmaster—
exposed as a true phony.

There is no <u>black</u> and <u>white</u>.
I don't fit in your tight little box.
This you cannot make right.
My ambiguity knocks.

There was nothing wrong
that needed to be fixed.

<u>Except you, that is.</u>

INVASION OF PRIVACY

Assuming is consuming—
just ask!
No need for accusing—
I wear no mask.

Addiction...
can be such a contradiction,
drugs are not the answer!
No, Bitch, they're your only conviction!

They are the plants that bring you closer—
to a more accepting God.
We're expected to keep composure,
but I find nothing quite as odd.

My freedom should not be threatened,
when all I need is peace.
Addiction shouldn't have been mentioned—
and you don't know better than me.

Finally breathing so easily,
it really is a blessing.
I won't act obscenely,
but it is sooo damn tempting!

Comparing me to a heroin addict.
is really quite funny.
But this I could not predict.
and the rage has left me hungry.

DMTakeshi

aLWAYs pAYiNG

Everyone has you lying
so they can get ahead.
I wasn't even trying...
and that, I truly regret.

Head of Family
Best of The Year
Growth So Rapidly
Changing to Persevere

For them.

But to want something for me—
so rude and so selfish.
I've lost my loyalty.
My future—just a blemish.

Whored myself for no return;
bit me, spanked me and scarred me.
For my life, they had no concern—
threw me over to discard me.

Unreadable

Tired of being your mat.
Tired of hurting.
Tired of following a path.
Tired of converting.

Ready to give up.
Ready to give zero fucks.
Ready to be corrupt.
Ready to <u>fucking</u> suck.

Y'all wore me out.
Y'all exploited me.
Y'all broke me and vowed
my torture's your ecstasy.

But I'm ready to give it all up.
Ready to give zero fucks.
So ready to be corrupt.
Ready to <u>fucking</u> suck.

We have an unhealthy relationship.
The world <u>fucks</u> me
and I always take that shit—
so graciously.

DMTakeshi

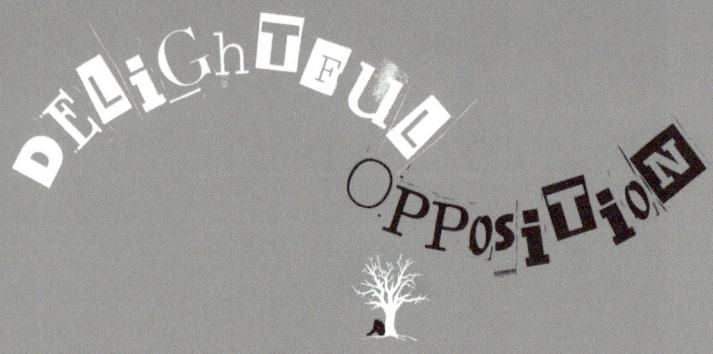

DELIGHTFUL OPPOSITION

When happiness is gross.
Not aiming for honorable.
Disgusted and it shows.
Just barely tolerable.

Relishing in everyone's misery.
Hoping your life is quite shitty.
For me there's no mystery,
and for you I have no pity.

Making this bliss absent
may seem like a chore.
I don't know what happened—
it's just not anymore.

Hating to cooperate—
my thirst for anger so great;
but I think the way you operate
is done in ways that aggravate.

Always a competition.
Don't fall silent.
Undesirable contradiction.
Unpredictable requirement.

When happiness can only translate to nasty.
Devotion for life ran away with my shame.
Now it's time to bask in my impurities—
and I'll just say you're to blame.

i HAVE NO FRiENds

I have no friends.
I stare at my lovely screen.
You'd call me a shut in.
For we've become very keen.

Writing my thoughts.
Fearing my ambitions.
And no one applauds.
They very rarely listen.

Am I the problem?
What have I caused?
My blow needs to soften.
Before I get tossed.

I have no friends.
The very definition of lonely.
Even my family pretends.
It's all my fault, mostly.

DMTakeshi

LAsT eXhaUsTEd BREaTh

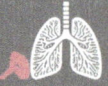

Heavy hearts.
Suffer in the lungs.
Feeling too much.
Left you gasping for air.
Loved in a way it's hard to deserve.
As a boulder rests on your chest.
Caring in a selfless way.
Led you to your last exhausted breath.

Unreadable

PLEASE, AND ThANK yoU

PLEASE. I don't know for how much longer.
PLEASE. I can keep my head above these waters.
Crying whispers in my mind,
"I just don't belong here."
Death isn't too far behind.
AND I NO LONGER FEAR.

PLEASE. I think this is my last chance.
PLEASE. I cannot break from this trance.
Soon I will feel the relief.
It only hurts for a bit.
Do not feel my grief.
You too will want to quit.

PLEASE. I can't let it go.
PLEASE. I couldn't say no.
I tried to say goodbye.
I was busy with a knife.
I'm sorry I needed to die.
I'm no longer in strife.

THANK YOU.
I am all better now.
THANK YOU.
I AM RELEASED.

DMTakeshi

COMFORTABLE TROUBLES

Torment blankets my heart.
It's never felt so good.
It won't try to restart.
And for all it has withstood.
I'm okay with falling apart.
Broken can't possibly be understood.

Nothing left meant to enter.
Permission to violate me granted.
Both arms raised in surrender.
My mind goes and leaves me stranded.
A promise that it won't get better.
This deep void only expanded.

BON VOYAGE

My mind begins to wander,
and my soul will soon follow.
I have a life to conquer—
for this hole, leaves me hollow.

Anchored in the abyss;
my frequencies, so recent.
There's nothing here to miss—
the tides are my greatest achievement.

Fantasies of past odysseys;
they cannot hold weight
when traveling new seas—
hastily fleeting, before it's too late.

Nothing holds me here,
the past lives, unfurled.
Now it is time to disappear—

"Bon Voyage, World."

DMTakeshi

iNsiGNiFicaNT BEiNG

Brutally trying to convey sentiment—
but I possess no real talent.
Causing outstanding detriment;
invariably inadequate.

I can only cause damage;
exploding my massacre.
No one can manage
something of this caliber.

Stay far, far away—
I'm a catastrophe
slowly spreading my decay,
and establishing my insanity.

I'm just an insignificant—
belittling is what I deserve.
My shame so insistent—
humiliation pierces the nerve.

Never merited affection.
Curses written in my stars.
I have absolutely no objection
to acquiring nasty scars.

I have never mattered,
and I have no meaning.
I've set the standard for...
an insignificant being.

NoT ShooTiNG FoR BETTeR

My life, it's here;
Riddled with poisons,
consumed in fear.

I hide my face so you can't see.
A COWARD and an IMPOSTER
built these walls too perfectly.
Most agree—it's improper.

Here, my life is, still.
Fears imprison my mind—
pain will fulfill,
and is never too far behind.

Declining sanity.
Aroused when anguished.
Such a gorgeous tragedy.
All reason vanquished.

Manifesting these words from my nightmares;
sharing my agonies with you—
only to find out no one cares,
devastation I can't undo.

Still, not shooting for better.

DMTakeshi

TiCK

Maybe if I could pick up this pen
I could set down these pills...
but I am pulled back in again,
Not equipped with the skills.

You asked what makes me tick,
something I never gave much thought.
I wanted to end it quick,
but it wasn't ever taught.

And if I were to tell the truth,
I would be fabricating that too.
No justice for forgotten youth,
unraveling all that you knew.

I was desperate for answers;
how do I create my own joy
when I find nothing matters?
Another enticing decoy.

Go home and rest your head.
Disregard that disturbing scene.
My toxicity—forcefully spread,
but we knew this was all foreseen.

I was always my biggest threat,
(and this wasn't just any dream)
my body kissed by death—
and once again—I've gone extreme.

DooM aNd GLooM

I don't want to go back,
I'd rather cry instead.
Life will always lack,
and I'm hanging by a thread.

Look at this huge mess—
painful arrest,
will not accept anything less;
only your best.

"I'm here all positive,
and you're all DOOM and GLOOM.
I just can't do it—
anymore with you."

You won't have to,
and I can make it easy.
Good night love.
By morning, I'll have left neatly.

DMTakeshi

RAMblinGs oF ME(NTaL iLLNEss)

I often romanticize about wanting to die...
Are you afraid?
—Or do you think you'd try?
                    Shh, we shouldn't talk like this—
                  it might be unhealthy to think like this.

...But did you hear what I said?

                  Of course I heard what you said.
I feel as though I am already dead.
The cuts no longer burn.
Deeper cuts the more blood shed.

                  What if we don't return?
Of course I'm scared.
Are you prepared?
                        Why now?
                        How to?
How could I?
            But, how could you?

CYCLICAL

Suicidal thoughts and suicidal prayers.
Suicidal hopes and suicidal nightmares.

Living this story everyday.
Just a tired cliché.

Weary and isolated.
Old and devastated.

Must keep proving.
Must keep fighting.
Must keep moving.

Forward,
onward and tortured.

For what?
So everything remains.

Suicidal thoughts and suicidal prayers.
Suicidal hopes and suicidal nightmares.

iF YoU oR soMEoNE YoU KNoW NEEds hELP...

The Trevor Project is here for you, day or night. The Trevor Project is the leading suicide prevention and crisis intervention nonprofit organization for LGBTQ+ young people. We provide information & support to LGBTQ+ young people 24/7, all year round.
https://chat.trvr.org/
<u>Chat With Us</u>
<u>Call Us: 1-866-488-7386</u>
<u>Text Us: 678-678</u>

iF YoU oR soMEoNE YoU KNoW NEEds hELP...

Suicide Prevention Hotline
call or text #988. Hours are available 24/7
and the cost is free.
OR
Text HOME to 741741 to reach a trained Crisis Counselor
through Crisis Text Line, a global not-for-profit
organization. Free, 24/7, confidential.

About the Author

My journey as a writer began at the tender age of seven when the magic of words first captured my imagination. My mother was a poetess and I admired every syllable, memorizing them as my own. From scribbled stories in notebooks to heartfelt poems penned in the quiet of night, writing became my sanctuary.

As the years unfolded, so did my passion for storytelling. Each word became a brushstroke on the canvas of my life, painting pictures of adventure, love, heartache, and resilience. I delved into the realms of poetry and prose exploring the nuances of language and the endless possibilities it held.

With every piece I crafted, I discovered more about myself and the world around me. Writing became not just a creative outlet but a journey of self-discovery, introspection, and growth. Through the highs and lows of life, my pen remained my constant companion, shaping my thoughts into narratives that resonated with others.

Today, as I look back on my journey, I am grateful for the gift of words and the privilege of sharing my stories with the world. My writing has been a reflection of my experiences, my dreams, and my evolving perspective on life.

Join me on this ongoing odyssey through words, where each page turned is a step closer to understanding ourselves and the beauty of the human experience.

With gratitude,
DM Takeshi

www.ingramcontent.com/pod-product-compliance
Lightning Source LLC
Chambersburg PA
CBHW041723070526
44585CB00006B/132